A Policy Guide to Steel Moment-frame Construction

SAC Joint Venture
a partnership of:
Structural Engineers Association of California (SEAOC)
Applied Technology Council (ATC)
California Universities for Research in Earthquake Engineering (CUREe)

Prepared for SAC Joint Venture by
Ronald O. Hamburger

Project Oversight Committee

William J. Hall, Chair

Shirin Ader
John M. Barsom
Roger Ferch
Theodore V. Galambos
John Gross
James R. Harris
Richard Holguin

Nestor Iwankiw
Roy G. Johnston
Len Joseph
Duane K. Miller
John Theiss
John H. Wiggins

SAC Project Management Committee

SEAOC: William T. Holmes
ATC: Christoper Rojahn
CUREe: Robin Shepherd

Program Manager: Stephen A. Mahin
Project Director for Topical Investigations:
James O. Malley
Project Director for Product Development:
Ronald O. Hamburger

SAC Joint Venture

Structural Engineers Association of California
www.seaoc.org

Applied Technology Council
www.atcouncil.org

California Universities for Research in Earthquake Engineering
www.curee.edu

November, 2000

DISCLAIMER

This document provides information on the seismic performance of steel moment-frame structures and the results and recommendations of an intensive research and development program that culminated in a series of engineering and construction criteria documents. It updates and replaces an earlier publication with the same title and is primarily intended to provide building owners, regulators, and policy makers with summary level information on the earthquake risk associated with steel moment-frame buildings, and measures that are available to address this risk. **No warranty is offered with regard to the recommendations contained herein, either by the Federal Emergency Management Agency, the SAC Joint Venture, the individual Joint Venture partners, or their directors, members or employees or consultants. These organizations and their employees do not assume any legal liability or responsibility for the accuracy, completeness, or usefulness of any of the information, products or processes included in this publication. The reader is cautioned to review carefully the material presented herein and exercise independent judgment as to its suitability for specific applications.** This publication has been prepared by the SAC Joint Venture with funding provided by the Federal Emergency Management Agency, under contract number EMW-95-C-4770.

Cover Art. The background photograph on the cover of this guide for Policy Makers is a cityscape of a portion of the financial district of the City of San Francisco. Each of the tall buildings visible in this cityscape is a steel moment-frame building. Similar populations of these buildings exist in most other American cities and many thousands of smaller steel moment-frame buildings are present around the United States as well. Until the 1994 Northridge earthquake, many engineers regarded these buildings as highly resistant to earthquake damage. The discovery of unanticipated fracturing of the steel framing following the 1994 Northridge earthquake shattered this belief and called to question the safety of these structures.

THE SAC JOINT VENTURE

SAC is a joint venture of the Structural Engineers Association of California (SEAOC), the Applied Technology Council (ATC), and California Universities for Research in Earthquake Engineering (CUREe), formed specifically to address both immediate and long-term needs related to solving performance problems with welded, steel moment-frame connections discovered following the 1994 Northridge earthquake. SEAOC is a professional organization composed of more than 3,000 practicing structural engineers in California. The volunteer efforts of SEAOC's members on various technical committees have been instrumental in the development of the earthquake design provisions contained in the *Uniform Building Code* and the 1997 *National Earthquake Hazards Reduction Program (NEHRP) Recommended Provisions for Seismic Regulations for New Buildings and Other Structures*. ATC is a nonprofit corporation founded to develop structural engineering resources and applications to mitigate the effects of natural and other hazards on the built environment. Since its inception in the early 1970s, ATC has developed the technical basis for the current model national seismic design codes for buildings; the *de-facto* national standard for post earthquake safety evaluation of buildings; nationally applicable guidelines and procedures for the identification, evaluation, and rehabilitation of seismically hazardous buildings; and other widely used procedures and data to improve structural engineering practice. CUREe is a nonprofit organization formed to promote and conduct research and educational activities related to earthquake hazard mitigation. CUREe's eight institutional members are the California Institute of Technology, Stanford University, the University of California at Berkeley, the University of California at Davis, the University of California at Irvine, the University of California at Los Angeles, the University of California at San Diego, and the University of Southern California. These university earthquake research laboratory, library, computer and faculty resources are among the most extensive in the United States. The SAC Joint Venture allows these three organizations to combine their extensive and unique resources, augmented by consultants and subcontractor universities and organizations from across the nation, into an integrated team of practitioners and researchers, uniquely qualified to solve problems related to the seismic performance of steel moment-frame structures.

ACKNOWLEDGEMENTS

Funding for Phases I and II of the SAC Steel Program to Reduce the Earthquake Hazards of Steel Moment-Frame Structures was principally provided by the Federal Emergency Management Agency, with ten percent of the Phase I program funded by the State of California, Office of Emergency Services. Substantial additional support, in the form of donated materials, services, and data has been provided by a number of individual consulting engineers, inspectors, researchers, fabricators, materials suppliers and industry groups. Special efforts have been made to maintain a liaison with the engineering profession, researchers, the steel industry, fabricators, code-writing organizations and model code groups, building officials, insurance and risk-management groups, and federal and state agencies active in earthquake hazard mitigation efforts. SAC wishes to acknowledge the support and participation of each of the above groups, organizations and individuals. In particular, we wish to acknowledge the contributions provided by the American Institute of Steel Construction, the Lincoln Electric Company, the National Institute of Standards and Technology, the National Science Foundation, and the Structural Shape Producers Council. SAC also takes this opportunity to acknowledge the efforts of the project participants – the managers, investigators, writers, and editorial and production staff – whose work has contributed to the development of these documents. Finally, SAC extends special acknowledgement to Mr. Michael Mahoney, FEMA Project Officer, and Dr. Robert Hanson, FEMA Technical Advisor, for their continued support and contribution to the success of this effort.

INTRODUCTION

The Northridge earthquake of January 17, 1994, caused widespread building damage throughout some of the most heavily populated communities of Southern California including the San Fernando Valley, Santa Monica and West Los Angeles, resulting in estimated economic losses exceeding $30 billion. Much of the damage sustained was quite predictable, occurring in types of buildings that engineers had previously identified as having low seismic resistance and significant risk of damage in earthquakes. This included older masonry and concrete buildings, but not steel framed buildings. Surprisingly, however, a number of modern, welded, steel, moment-frame buildings also sustained significant damage. This damage consisted of a brittle fracturing of the steel frames at the welded joints between the beams (horizontal framing members) and columns (vertical framing members). A few of the most severely damaged buildings could readily be observed to be out-of-plumb (leaning to one side). However, many of the damaged buildings exhibited no outward signs of these fractures, making damage detection both difficult and costly. Then, exactly one year later, on January 17, 1995, the city of Kobe, Japan also experienced a large earthquake, causing similar unanticipated damage to steel moment-frame buildings.

Following discovery of hidden damage in Los Angeles area buildings, the potential for similar, undiscovered damage in San Francisco and other communities affected by past earthquakes was raised.

Ventura Boulevard in the San Fernando Valley. Many of these buildings had hidden damage.

Prior to the 1994 Northridge and 1995 Kobe earthquakes, engineers believed that steel moment-frames would behave in a ductile manner, bending under earthquake loading, but not breaking. As a result, this became one of the most common types of construction used for major buildings in areas subject to severe earthquakes. The discovery of the potential for fracturing in these frames called to question the adequacy of the building code provisions dealing with this type of construction and created a crisis of confidence around the world. Engineers did not have clear guidance on how to detect damage, repair the damage they found, assess the safety of existing buildings, upgrade buildings found to be deficient or design new steel moment-frame structures to perform adequately in earthquakes. The observed damage also raised questions as to whether buildings in cities affected by other past earthquakes had sustained similar undetected damage and were now weakened and potentially hazardous. In fact, some structures in the San Francisco Bay area have been discovered to have similar fracture damage most probably dating to the 1989 Loma Prieta earthquake.

In response to the many concerns raised by these damage discoveries, the Federal Emergency Management Agency (FEMA) sponsored a program of directed investigation and development to identify the cause of the damage, quantify the risk inherent in steel structures and develop practical and effective engineering criteria for mitigation of this risk. FEMA contracted with the SAC Joint Venture, a partnership of the Structural Engineers Association of California (SEAOC), a professional association with more than 3,000 members; the Applied Technology Council (ATC), a non-profit foundation dedicated to the translation of structural engineering research into state-of-art practice guidelines; and the California Universities for Research in Earthquake Engineering (CUREe), a consortium of eight California universities with comprehensive earthquake engineering research facilities and personnel. The resulting FEMA/SAC project was conducted over a period of 6 years at a cost of $12 million and included the participation of hundreds of leading practicing engineers, university researchers, industry associations, contractors, materials suppliers, inspectors and building officials from around the United States. These efforts were coordinated with parallel efforts conducted by other agencies, including the National Science Foundation and National Institute of Standards and Technology (NIST), and with concurrent efforts in other nations, including a large program in Japan. In all, hundreds of tests of material specimens and large-scale structural assemblies were conducted, as well as thousands of computerized analytical investigations.

As the project progressed, interim guidance documents were published to provide practicing engineers and the construction industry with important information on the lessons learned, as well as recommendations for investigation, repair, upgrade, and design of steel moment-frame buildings. Many of these recommendations have already been incorporated into recent building codes. This project culminated with the publication of four engineering practice guideline documents. These four volumes include state-of-the-art recommendations that should be included in future building codes, as well as guidelines that may be applied voluntarily to assess and reduce the earthquake risk in our communities.

This policy guide has been prepared to provide a nontechnical summary of the valuable information contained in the FEMA/SAC publications, an understanding of the risk associated with steel moment-frame buildings, and the practical measures that can be taken to reduce this risk. It is anticipated that this guide will be of interest to building owners and tenants, members of the financial and insurance industries, and to government planners and the building regulation community.

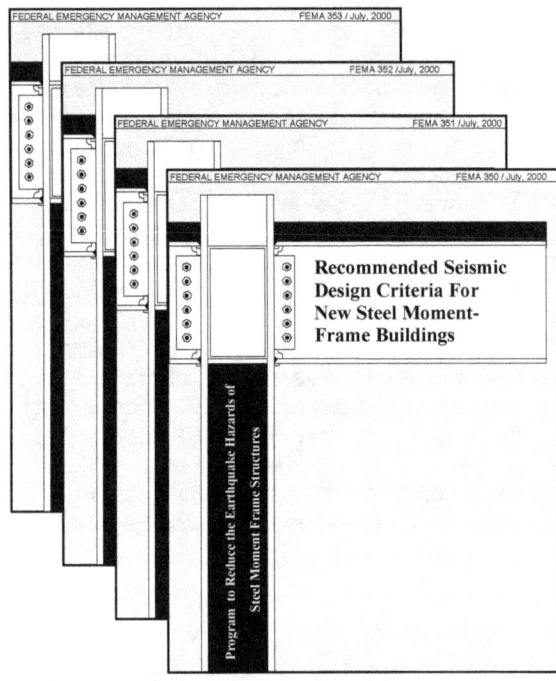

FEMA 350 Recommended Seismic Design Criteria for New Steel Moment-Frame Buildings

FEMA 351 Recommended Seismic Evaluation and Upgrade Criteria for Existing Welded Steel Moment-Frame Buildings

FEMA 352 Recommended Post-earthquake Evaluation and Repair Criteria for Welded Steel Moment-Frame Buildings

FEMA 353 Recommended Specifications and Quality Assurance Guidelines for Steel Moment-Frame Construction for Seismic Applications

AN OVERVIEW OF THE PROBLEM

What is a steel moment-frame building?

All steel-framed buildings derive basic structural support for the building weight from a skeleton (or frame) composed of horizontal steel beams and vertical steel columns. In addition to being able to support vertical loads, including the weight of the building itself and the contents, structures must also be able to resist lateral (horizontal) forces produced by wind and earthquakes. In some steel frame structures, this lateral resistance is derived from the presence of diagonal braces or masonry or concrete walls. In steel moment-frame buildings, the ends of the beams are rigidly joined to the columns so that the buildings can resist lateral wind and earthquake forces without the assistance of additional braces or walls. This style of construction is very popular for many building occupancies, because the absence of diagonal braces and structural walls allows complete freedom for interior space layout and aesthetic exterior expression.

Construction of a modern steel frame building in which the ends of beams are rigidly joined to columns by welded connections.

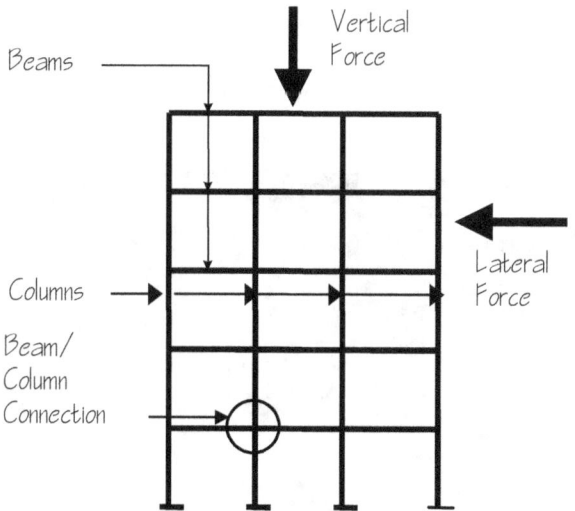

A steel moment-frame is an assembly of beams and columns, rigidly joined together to resist both vertical and lateral forces.

Are all steel moment-frame buildings vulnerable to the type of damage that occurred in the Northridge earthquake?

The steel moment-frame buildings damaged in the 1994 Northridge earthquake are a special type, known as welded steel moment-frames (WSMF). This is because the beams and columns in these structures are connected with welded joints. WSMF construction first became popular in the 1960s. In earlier buildings, the connections between the beams and columns were either bolted or riveted. While these older buildings also may be vulnerable to earthquake damage, they did not experience the type of connection fractures discovered following the Northridge earthquake. Generally, welded steel moment-frame buildings constructed in the period 1964-1994 should be considered vulnerable to this damage. Buildings constructed after 1994 and incorporating connection design and fabrication practices recommended by the FEMA/SAC program are anticipated to have significantly less vulnerability.

What does the damage consist of?

The damage discovered in WSMF buildings consists of a fracturing, or cracking, of the welded connections between the beams and columns that form the frame, or skeleton, of the structure. This damage occurs most commonly at the welded joint between a column and the bottom flange of a beam. Once a crack has started, it can continue in any of several different patterns and in some cases has been found to completely sever beams or columns.

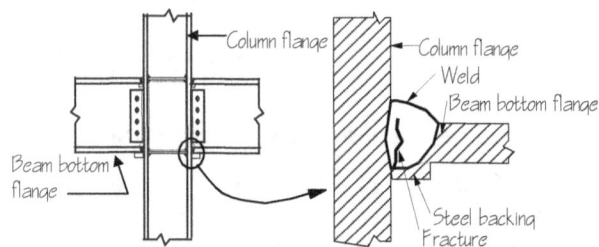

Damage consists of fractures or cracks that initiate in the welded joints of the beams to columns.

Damage ranges from small cracks that are difficult to see, to much larger cracks. Here, a crack began at the weld and progressed into the column flange, withdrawing a divot of material.

What does the damage look like?

There are several common types of damage, each of which looks somewhat different. The most common cracks initiate in the weld itself or just next to the weld. These cracks often are very thin and difficult to see. In a few cases, cracks cannot be seen at all. In some cases, cracks cause large scoop-like pieces of the column flange, called divots, to be pulled out. In still other cases, the cracks run across the entire column, practically dividing it into two unconnected pieces.

What is the effect of the damage?

WSMF buildings rely on the connections between their beams and columns to resist wind and earthquake loads. When the welded joints that form these connections break, the building loses some of the strength and stiffness it needs to resist these loads. The magnitude and significance of this capacity loss depends on the unique design and construction attributes of each building, as well as the extent and type of damage sustained. Few buildings were damaged so severely in the Northridge earthquake that they represented imminent collapse hazards. However, significant weakening of some buildings did occur. Once the welded joints fracture, other types of damage can also occur including damage to bolted joints. Damage that results in the complete severing of beams or columns or their connections poses a serious problem and could result in the potential for localized collapse.

Fracturing of welded connections can lead to damage to the bolted connections that hold the beams onto the columns, creating potential for localized collapse.

Why did this damage occur?

We now understand that the vulnerability of WSMF structures is a result of a number of inter-related factors. Early research, conducted in the 1960s and 70s suggested that a particular style of connection could perform adequately. Designers then routinely began to specify this connection in their designs. However, the particular style of connection tends to concentrate high stresses at some of the weakest points in the assembly, and in fact, some of the early research showed some potential vulnerability. As the cost of construction labor increased, relative to the price of construction materials, engineers adopted designs that minimized the number of connections in each building, resulting in larger members and increased loads on the connections. At the same time, the industry adopted a type of welding that could be used to make these connections more quickly, but sometimes resulted in welds that were more susceptible to cracking. Although building codes required that inspectors ensure the quality of this welding, the inspection techniques and procedures used were often not adequate. Finally, the steel industry found new ways to economically produce structural steel with higher strength. Although the steel became stronger, designers were unaware of this and continued to specify the same connections. Often, these connections did not have adequate strength to match the newer steel material and were therefore, even more vulnerable. In the end, the typical connections used in WSMF buildings were just not adequate to withstand the severe demands produced by an earthquake.

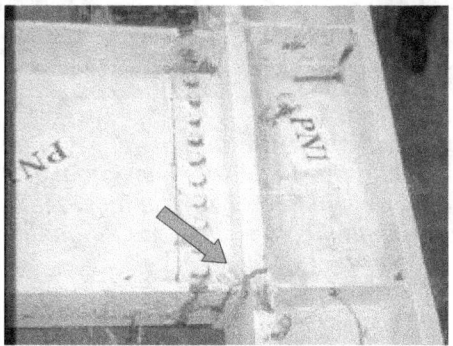

Fractures commonly initiate at the welded joint of the beam bottom flange to column.

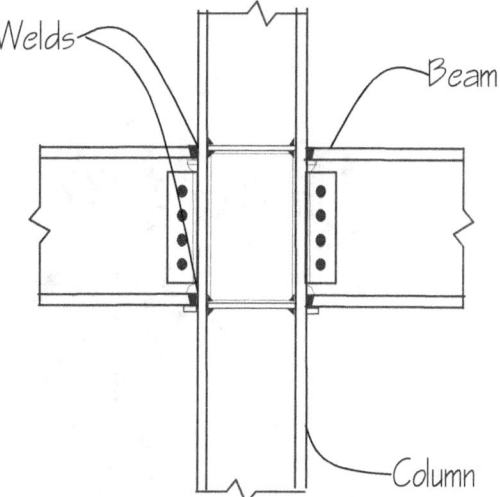

The typical connection used prior to 1994. Severe stress concentrations inherent in its configuration were not considered in the design.

How widespread was this damage?

Although no comprehensive survey of all of the steel buildings affected by the Northridge earthquake has been conducted, the City of Los Angeles did enact an ordinance that required mandatory inspection of nearly 200 buildings in areas that experienced the most intense ground shaking. Initial reports from this mandatory inspection program erroneously indicated that nearly every one of these buildings had experienced damage and in some cases, that this damage was extensive. It was projected that perhaps thousands of buildings had been damaged. It is now known that damage was much less widespread than originally thought and that many of the conditions that were originally identified as damage actually were imperfections in the original construction work. Of the nearly 200 buildings that were inspected under the City of Los Angeles ordinance, it now appears that only about 1/3 had any actual earthquake damage and that more than 90% of the total damage discovered occurred within a small group of approximately 30 buildings. Therefore, although this damage was significant, and does warrant a change in the design and construction practices prevalent prior to 1994, it appears that the risk of severe damage to buildings is relatively slight, except under very intense ground shaking.

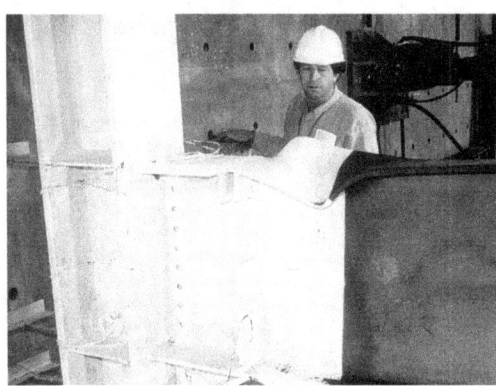

Engineers expect steel to be ductile, capable of extensive bending and deformation without fracturing, as shown in this test specimen. The development of cracks in the steel at relatively low levels of loading was unexpected.

Why was this damage a surprise?

In its basic form, steel is a very ductile material, able to undergo extensive deformation and distortion before breaking. This is the type of behavior desired for earthquake resistance, so engineers believed WSMF buildings would be quite earthquake resistant. Following the 1971 San Fernando earthquake, the 1987 Whittier Narrows earthquake, and the 1989 Loma Prieta earthquake, there were few reports of significant damage to steel buildings, especially as compared to other types of construction, confirming this general belief. However, relatively few WSMF buildings were subjected to severe ground motion in these events. As the industry's confidence in the ability of WSMF buildings to resist earthquake damage grew, design practice, material production processes and construction techniques changed, adding unexpected vulnerability. The 1994 Northridge earthquake was the first event in which a large number of recently constructed WSMF buildings were subjected to strong ground motion.

Have other earthquakes caused similar damage?

When damaged WSMF buildings were first discovered following the Northridge earthquake, there was speculation that this was a result of some peculiar characteristic of the earthquake itself or of local design and construction practices in the Los Angeles region. It has now been confirmed that similar damage occurred to some buildings affected by the 1989 Loma Prieta earthquake and also the 1992 Landers and Big Bear earthquakes. In 1995, the Kobe earthquake resulted in damage to several hundred steel buildings, and the collapse of 50 older steel buildings. Japanese researchers have confirmed problems similar to those experienced in the Northridge earthquake. Engineering researchers around the world have recognized this behavior as a common problem for welded steel moment-frame buildings designed and constructed using practices prevalent prior to the Northridge earthquake and have been working together to find solutions.

Many steel moment-frame buildings were damaged in the 1995 Kobe earthquake. The building shown here, lying on its side, is one of more than 50 older steel buildings that collapsed.

How many WSMF buildings are there?

Thousands of WSMF buildings have been constructed in all regions of the United States. One of the factors contributing to the seriousness of this problem is that WSMF construction is often used in many of the nation's most important facilities, including hospital buildings, emergency command centers and other federal, state and local government office buildings. It is commonly used for commercial office structures. Most high-rise buildings constructed in the United States in the last 30 years incorporate this type of construction. WSMF construction has also frequently been used for mid-rise and to a lesser extent, low-rise commercial and institutional construction, auditoriums and other assembly occupancies, and has seen limited application in industrial facilities. It is relatively uncommon in residential construction, although some high-rise condominium type buildings are of this construction type.

Many of the tallest buildings in our major cities are of WSMF construction.

Are existing WSMF structures safe?

No structure is absolutely safe and, if subjected to sufficiently large loads, a structure made of any material will collapse. Building codes in the United States permit structures to be damaged by strong earthquakes, but attempt to prevent collapse for the most severe levels of ground motion which can be expected at the site. No WSMF structure in the United States has ever collapsed as a result of earthquake loading. However, research conducted as part of the FEMA/SAC project confirms that WSMF structures with the style of beam-column connection typically used prior to the Northridge earthquake have a higher risk of earthquake-induced collapse than desired for new buildings.

How does the risk of WSMF structures compare to other types of buildings?

Many other types of buildings present much greater risks of collapse than do WSMF buildings. Based on observations from past earthquakes, buildings that present greater risks include buildings of unreinforced masonry construction, buildings of concrete and masonry construction that pre-date the mid-1970s, buildings of precast concrete construction and even some types of wood frame construction. However, many WSMF buildings are large and house many occupants. The earthquake-induced collapse of one such structure could result in a very large and unacceptable life loss.

Older concrete frame, tilt-up and masonry buildings are generally more prone to earthquake-induced collapse than WSMF buildings.

AFTER THE NEXT EARTHQUAKE

Can one tell if a WSMF building is damaged?

Some damaged WSMF buildings permanently lean to one side after an earthquake and have severe damage to finishes, providing a clear indication that the building has sustained structural damage. However, many WSMF buildings do not exhibit any obvious signs of damage. To determine if these buildings are damaged, it is necessary to conduct an engineering inspection of the framing and connections. To conduct these inspections, it is necessary first to remove building finishes and fireproofing. These inspections can be disruptive of occupancy and very expensive, ranging from a few hundred dollars to more than one thousand dollars per connection. Large buildings may have several thousand connections. The presence of asbestos, sometimes used in fireproofing in buildings constructed prior to 1979, substantially increases the inspection costs.

The most severely damaged buildings will often lean to one side. However, there may be no obvious indications of the damage in some buildings.

Is it safe to occupy a damaged building?

If a building is severely damaged, there is a risk that aftershocks or subsequent strong winds or earthquakes may cause partial or total collapse of the building. The more severe the damage, the higher this risk. Most buildings damaged by the Northridge earthquake were judged to be safe for continued occupancy while repairs were made. *FEMA 352* provides engineering procedures that can be used by building officials and engineers to quantify the risk associated with continued occupancy of damaged buildings. FEMA 352 also provides recommendations as to when a building should be deemed unsafe for further occupancy.

How does an owner know if a building is safe?

Following an earthquake, building departments will typically perform rapid inspections of affected buildings to identify buildings that may be unsafe. Once such an inspection has been performed, the building department will typically post the building with a placard that indicates whether the building is safe for occupancy. *FEMA 352* provides procedures that building officials can use to conduct these rapid inspections. If the building department doesn't provide this service, building owners can retain private engineers or inspection firms for this purpose.

Is the building department inspection enough?

Rapid inspections conducted by building departments after an earthquake are intended to identify those buildings at greatest risk of endangering the public safety. They are not adequate to detect all damage a building has sustained. If a building has experienced strong ground motion, the building owner should retain an engineer to conduct more thorough inspections in accordance with *FEMA 352*, even if the building department posts the building as safe.

After an earthquake, is it necessary to inspect every WSMF building?

The amount of damage sustained by a building is closely related to the severity of ground motion at the building site. Unless a building experiences strong ground motion, it is unlikely that it will sustain significant damage. *FEMA 352* recommends that all buildings thought to have experienced ground motion in excess of certain levels be subjected to detailed inspections to determine if they sustained significant damage. Because detailed inspections can be time consuming and costly, *FEMA 352* also recommends that an initial, rapid investigation be performed to look for obvious signs of severe damage that could pose an immediate threat to life safety.

Is it necessary to inspect every connection in a building?

The only way to ensure that all damage in a structure is found is to inspect all of the connections. However, as previously discussed, connection inspections are costly and disruptive. Therefore most owners would prefer not to inspect every connection, if possible. Because damage tends to be distributed throughout a structure, it is possible to inspect a sample of the total number of connections in a building and make judgments as to how widespread damage is likely to be throughout the entire building. *FEMA 352* provides recommendations for selecting an appropriate sample and drawing conclusions on the condition of the building, based on the damage found in the sample.

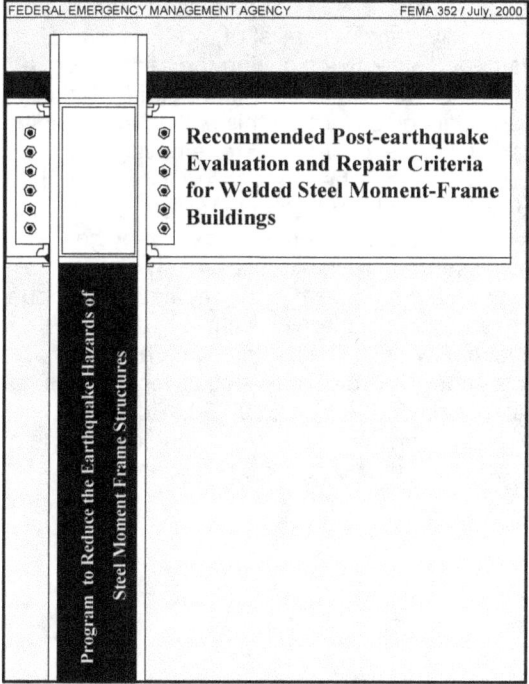

FEDERAL EMERGENCY MANAGEMENT AGENCY   FEMA 352 / July, 2000

Recommended Post-earthquake Evaluation and Repair Criteria for Welded Steel Moment-Frame Buildings

Program to Reduce the Earthquake Hazards of Steel Moment Frame Structures

FEMA 352 contains recommended procedures for identifying earthquake damage in WSMF buildings and the risk of continued occupancy.

Is it possible to repair any damaged building?

It is technically possible to repair almost any damaged building. However, if a building is severely damaged, the cost of repair may exceed the replacement cost. Repair may be particularly difficult and costly if a building has experienced large, permanent sideways displacement, sometimes called drift. In such cases, the structure may even be unsafe for occupancy even for repair. In these cases, it may make more sense to demolish a building and replace it rather than to repair it. Following the 1994 Northridge earthquake, the owner of one building elected to do this.

How is the fracture damage repaired?

Each type of fracture requires a somewhat different repair procedure. *FEMA 352* provides recommendations for many types of repair. Generally, repairs consist of local removal of the damaged steel using cutting torches or electric arcs, and welding new, undamaged material back in its place. To do this cutting and welding safely, it is necessary first to remove any combustible finishes from the work area and also to provide ventilation to remove potentially harmful fumes. In some cases, it may be necessary to provide temporary shoring of the damaged element while the repair work is done. These operations are disruptive to normal occupancy of the immediate work area and also quite costly. Typical connection repair costs can range from $10,000 to $20,000. Additional costs are associated with the temporary loss of use of floor space during repair operations.

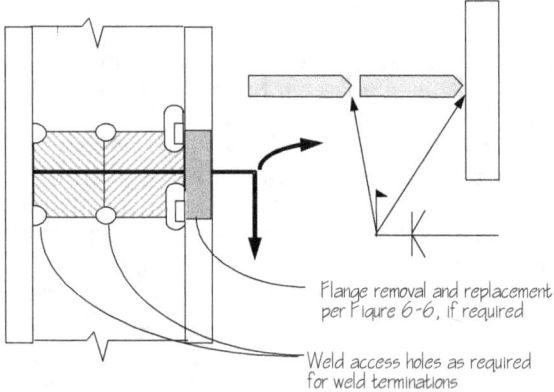

Flange removal and replacement per Figure 6-6, if required

Weld access holes as required for weld terminations

FEMA 352 provides detailed repair procedures for different types of damage. One repair procedure is shown here as an example.

DEALING WITH THE RISK OF EXISTING BUILDINGS

Is it possible to upgrade an existing WSMF building?

It is technically feasible to upgrade an existing steel moment-frame building and improve its probable performance in future earthquakes. The most common methods are upgrades of the individual connections, addition of steel braces, concrete or masonry walls, or addition of energy dissipation systems. Each of these approaches may offer advantages in particular buildings.

Buildings can be upgraded by modifying connections, adding braces and other methods.

What is a connection upgrade?

Connection upgrades are the most direct approach to improving the seismic performance of an existing steel moment-frame structure. As previously discussed, existing connections can fracture because their shape results in the development of large stress concentrations; some welds have large defects that reduce their strength and the weld metal itself may be of low toughness and unable to resist the large stresses imposed on it. Connection upgrades address these problems directly by modifying the shape of the connection to reduce the stress concentrations. In addition, depending on the approach used, the upgrade may include replacement of defective welds and welds with low toughness with new welds that have improved toughness and better workmanship. *FEMA 351* provides information and design criteria for a number of alternative methods of upgrading connections.

Connections can be upgraded by welding or bolting new plates onto the beams and columns to change the connection shape and reduce stress concentrations. In some cases, it may also be appropriate to replace defective welds and welds with low toughness with welds with improved toughness and workmanship.

How does the addition of braces or walls upgrade a building?

Connection fractures occur when the force delivered by the earthquake exceeds the connection strength or when connection elements experience low-cycle fatigue. This is similar to what happens to a paper clip, when it is bent back and forth repeatedly. As the metal is bent back and forth, it dissipates energy, but also becomes damaged. Eventually, so much damage occurs that the metal breaks. If a connection is bent through a large angle of deformation, or is relatively weak or brittle, it may only be able to withstand one or two cycles, that is, be bent back and forth once or twice. However, if the bending deformation is relatively small, or if the connection material has high toughness, the connection may be able to withstand a number of such cycles. Earthquakes produce many cycles of motion.

When steel braces or masonry or concrete walls are added to a building, they stiffen it and reduce the amount that the building will sway in an earthquake. This reduces the amount of bending on the connections. Guidance on the use of these techniques is already available in such publications as *FEMA-273, NEHRP Guidelines for Seismic Rehabilitation of Buildings* and, therefore, is not repeated in *FEMA 351*.

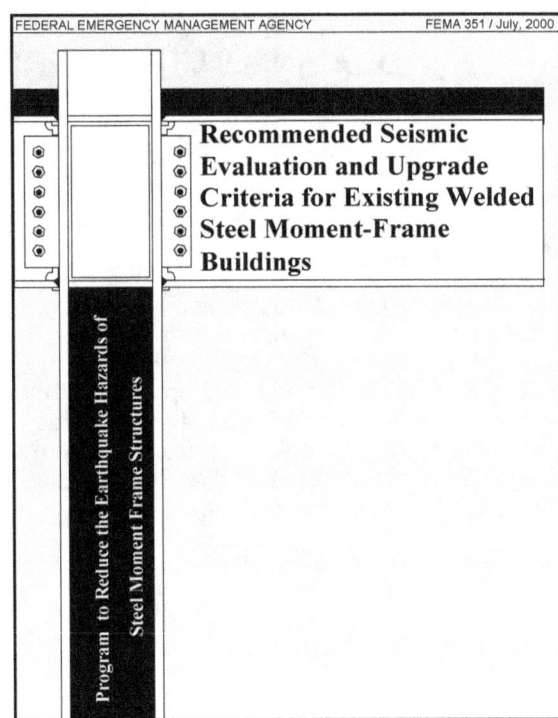

Recommended Seismic Evaluation and Upgrade Criteria for Existing Welded Steel Moment-Frame Buildings

Program to Reduce the Earthquake Hazards of Steel Moment Frame Structures

FEMA 351 provides engineering procedures for evaluating the probable performance of buildings in future earthquakes. These procedures address the safety as well as financial aspects of earthquake performance.

What is an energy dissipation system?

Energy dissipation systems reduce the amount that buildings sway in an earthquake by converting the earthquake's energy into heat. Several types of energy dissipation devices are available. One type is a hydraulic cylinder, similar to the shock absorbers in an automobile. Other types dissipate energy through friction. In order for these systems to be effective, one end of the device must move relative to the other end. The most common way to do this is to install the dissipation devices as part of a bracing system between the building floors. As the building sways in an earthquake and one floor moves relative to another, this drives the device and dissipates the energy as heat. Detailed guidance on the design of energy dissipation systems is already available in such documents as *FEMA 273 NEHRP Guidelines for Seismic Rehabilitation of Buildings* and, therefore, is not covered in detail in the steel moment-frame criteria documents.

Energy dissipation systems are typically installed in buildings as part of a vertical bracing system that extends between the building's floors.

What type of upgrade is best?

No one type of upgrade is best for all buildings. Basic factors that affect selection of an optimal alternative include the individual building's characteristics, the severity of motion anticipated at the building site, desired building performance, cost of the upgrade, the feasibility of performing upgrade work while the building remains occupied, and the effect of the upgrade on building appearance and space utilization. Addition of diagonal bracing may be the least costly alternative; however, its effect on building appearance and functionality may be viewed by some owners as unacceptable. Addition of energy dissipation devices will result in better performance of the building, but may cost more. Modification of individual connections would have the least effect on building appearance, but would inconvenience the existing tenants more than some other approaches and may cost more to implement.

How does an owner pick an appropriate upgrade approach?

To determine the best method of upgrading a building, an owner should retain an engineer to evaluate the building's probable earthquake performance. An upgrade should be considered if the probable performance is unacceptable. In the absence of ordinances that require upgrade of buildings, it will be necessary for each owner to decide what constitutes acceptable performance. The engineer can assist the owner in understanding the various options. Once a performance objective is selected, the engineer can prepare preliminary designs for various upgrade approaches, together with estimates of probable construction cost. The owner can then select the most appropriate design considering the cost, structural performance improvements, aesthetics and other impacts of each upgrade approach on the building.

Should all existing WSMF buildings be upgraded?

A building should be upgraded only if the risk of losses associated with its probable performance in future earthquakes is deemed unacceptable. Individual owners may make this judgement, or in some cases, the local community may decide that risk is unacceptable. The severity of earthquake risk associated with a building's performance in future earthquakes, as well as the acceptability of this risk, must be determined on a building-specific basis. The earthquake performance of some WSMF buildings housing critical occupancies and located in zones likely to experience frequent intense ground motion may be unacceptable, whereas many other WSMF buildings will be capable of performing adequately in the levels of ground motion they are likely to experience. To determine if a building should be upgraded, an owner should retain the services of an engineer to evaluate the building's probable performance in future earthquakes, permitting the owner to balance the assessed risks against the cost of mitigation.

What is the cost of upgrading a WSMF?

Upgrade costs are dependent on a number of factors including the upgrade approach selected, the structural configuration of the building, the specific seismic deficiencies present, the severity of earthquake motion used as a basis for design, the intended performance of the upgraded building, the building's occupancy, and the nature of tenant improvements and furnishings. Costs can range from about $10 per square foot of building floor area to as much as $30 or more. This can be compared to the typical costs associated with new building construction. Exclusive of the costs of land acquisition, planning and design, the construction cost of a new steel frame building shell will range from about $70 to $125 per square foot. The cost of tenant improvements, including interior partitions, ceilings, lighting, and furnishings can equal the building construction costs.

When is the best time to upgrade?

Much of the cost of performing a seismic upgrade relates to the need to demolish and restore architectural finishes and to displace tenants temporarily from construction work areas. In many commercial buildings these costs are incurred on a regular, periodic basis as leases expire and tenants in a building change. Therefore, the most economical time to perform an upgrade is during a change of tenant occupancy. Most buildings have many tenants with staggered lease periods. If upgrade work is to be done when tenant space is being changed from one leaseholder to the next, it will usually be necessary to phase the work over a period of years. If such an approach is taken, the probable performance of the building in the event that an earthquake occurs while it is only partially upgraded should be evaluated for each of the potential stages of completion, to ensure that an unsafe condition is not created inadvertently. Another beneficial time to perform upgrade work is at the time of property transfer. If upgrade work is done as part of a building ownership transfer, financing can include additional funding to perform the upgrade work.

Is upgrading economically feasible?

The feasibility of an upgrade depends on the individual economic circumstances of each building, its tenants and owners. Earthquakes are infrequent events. Even in areas of high seismic risk, like California, most buildings will experience at most only one or perhaps two damaging earthquakes over their lives. Seismic upgrades can greatly reduce the financial and life losses that occur as a result of such earthquakes. However, because the probability of occurrence of a damaging earthquake is usually small, the present value of these avoided losses rarely exceeds the initial cost of the upgrade unless there are large life loss or occupancy interruption costs associated with the potential damage. If upgrades are performed concurrently with other building renovation work, such as remodeling or asbestos removal, the upgrade work will cost less and produce a more attractive return on the investment.

How can an owner evaluate a building's probable future performance?

To determine the probable performance of a building in future earthquakes, an owner should retain an engineer. *FEMA 351* provides structural engineers with several methods for evaluating the probable performance of buildings in future earthquakes. These methods include Simplified Loss Estimation, Detailed Loss Estimation and Detailed Performance Evaluation, a procedure that is compatible with modern performance-based design approaches.

How can an owner tell if a building will be safe in future earthquakes?

FEMA 351 presents engineering procedures that can be used to estimate the probability that a building will experience life-threatening damage in future earthquakes. The ability of a building to resist earthquakes without endangering life is dependent on two primary factors, the capacity of the building and the intensity of future earthquake ground motion. It must be remembered that any building has the potential to experience life-threatening damage, if it experiences sufficiently intense ground motion. In typical regions with significant earthquake risk, earthquakes that produce low levels of ground motion may be felt relatively frequently, perhaps one time every ten to twenty years. Such ground motion rarely causes damage. Intense ground motion, capable of causing severe damage to modern buildings, will occur much less frequently, perhaps only one time in a few hundred to a few thousand years. The procedures of *FEMA 351* allow determination of the probability that a building will experience either partial or total collapse, if earthquake ground motion of a specified intensity occurs. To use this method, the owner and engineer must agree upon an appropriate return period for the ground motion to be used as a basis for the evaluation. The return period is the average number of years, for example, 100, 500, etc., between damage-causing earthquakes.

What is the Simplified Loss Estimation Methodology?

The Simplified Loss Estimation Methodology contained in *FEMA 351* consists of a series of graphs that indicate the probability that WSMF buildings will experience various levels of damage if they are subjected to certain levels of ground motion. These graphs were compiled from data obtained for buildings in the Los Angeles area following the 1994 Northridge earthquake. To use these graphs, an engineer must estimate an intensity of ground motion to which a building will be subjected. Using the graph, an engineer can obtain an estimate of the percentage of the building's connections that will be damaged and the probable cost of connection repairs, if the building experiences an earthquake of a certain intensity. These graphs do not take into account the individual characteristics of a building, except in an approximate manner and, therefore, do not provide precise estimates. Rather, they provide an indication of the potential range of damage and repair costs and the probability that damage and repair costs will exceed certain amounts, based on the behavior of the buildings that were affected by the Northridge earthquake.

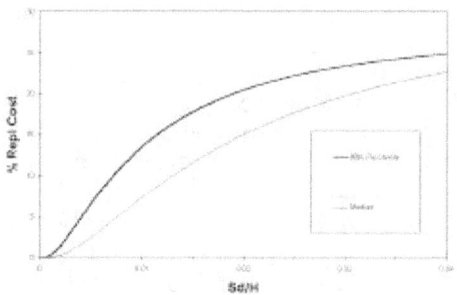

The Simplified Loss Estimation Methodology uses a series of graphs to relate probable earthquake losses to ground motion intensity.

What is the Detailed Loss Estimation Methodology?

In addition to the Simplified Loss Estimation Methodology, *FEMA 351* also presents a procedure for developing building-specific, damage and loss estimates for WSMF buildings. This method can be implemented in HAZUS, FEMA's nationally applicable loss estimation model, to explore the potential benefits to a community of requiring upgrade of steel buildings. The method can also be used to develop loss estimates for individual buildings to assist owners in making upgrade decisions. Loss estimates generated using this technique take into consideration the specific characteristics of individual buildings and, therefore, provide a more accurate basis for cost-benefit studies for seismic upgrades. However, the method is somewhat complex and requires specialized expertise and training to implement.

How safe should an existing building be?

There is no single commonly accepted minimum level of safety for existing buildings. However, it is always useful to compare the safety of an existing building with that intended for new buildings as well as with that of other existing buildings. New buildings are designed to provide a high level of confidence, on the order of 90%, that they will survive the most severe ground motion likely to be experienced, every 1,000 to 2,500 years, without collapse. Therefore, it is unlikely that most new buildings would ever experience earthquake-induced collapse. Most existing buildings will not be capable of providing the same performance as a new building. An existing building may be acceptably safe if it can provide high confidence that it will resist collapse under ground motion intensities likely to occur every 500 years or so. The selection of an acceptable level of safety depends on a number of factors including the number of occupants in the building, and its use. *FEMA 351* presents evaluation procedures that can be used to estimate the probability that a building will collapse in future earthquake ground motion and to associate a confidence level with this estimate.

Will it be possible to reuse a building after an earthquake?

In addition to safety concerns, many owners and tenants in buildings are concerned with their ability to return to a building after an earthquake, and continue to live or work in it. *FEMA 351* provides an evaluation procedure that may be used to determine the probability that a building will experience so much damage that it should not be reoccupied following an earthquake. To use this procedure, it is necessary for the owner and the engineer to select an appropriate return period for the ground motion upon which this evaluation will be based and the performance that will be acceptable if this ground motion occurs.

Is it cost effective to upgrade?

While earthquakes can cause catastrophic damage, in most cases the probability that a building will be affected by such an event is low. Even in the most seismically active regions of California, ground motions likely to cause substantial damage to WSMF buildings are currently projected to affect a building site only one time every hundred years or so. Given that many investors retain ownership in a building asset for a relatively small number of years, the likelihood that a loss will actually occur during an ownership period is low. Therefore, when owners balance the cost of a seismic upgrade program against the probable economic benefit to be gained during their ownership period, a good return on investment is often found to exist only if post-earthquake occupancy of a building is perceived to be critical for economic or other reasons, or if life loss is anticipated and the economic value of such loss is included in the evaluation.

Why is building performance expressed in probabilities?

The amount of damage that a building will sustain in an earthquake depends on a number of factors including the configuration and strength of the building, the quality of its construction, and the specific characteristics of the ground motion produced by the earthquake. Although engineers can develop estimates of each of these factors, it is not possible to predict any of these things precisely. Therefore, engineers must express future building performance in probabilistic terms.

Should communities adopt mandatory upgrade programs for steel frame buildings?

Given the low benefit/cost ratio for seismic upgrade of steel frame buildings, it is unlikely that many owners will perform such upgrades voluntarily. Mandatory upgrade ordinances can be an effective measure to assure that these buildings are upgraded. For example, a number of California cities, including Los Angeles and San Francisco, have successfully implemented ordinances requiring upgrade of unreinforced masonry buildings, a type of building that can collapse in even moderate earthquakes. However, similar ordinances requiring upgrade of WSMF buildings may not be an effective application of the limited resources available to a community. It is likely that other financial and health risks faced by the community are more significant than the hazards posed by the earthquake performance of steel frame buildings. Indeed, many communities have large inventories of buildings that are far more hazardous than typical steel frame buildings, including unreinforced masonry buildings and older concrete buildings. Before adopting a mandatory upgrade ordinance for steel frame buildings, communities should carefully consider the costs and benefits on a community-wide basis and weigh these against other potential applications of the limited resources available. FEMA's HAZUS loss estimation model is available to communities and can be used to provide guidance in deciding on the advisability of adopting a mandatory upgrade ordinance.

CRITERIA FOR NEW BUILDING DESIGN

How should new buildings be designed?

Buildings must be designed to meet minimum criteria specified in building codes. Model building codes are developed on a national basis by professional organizations representing engineers, architects, building officials and fire marshals, and are adopted, sometimes with modification, by individual cities, counties and states. Prior to the 1994 Northridge earthquake, the building codes contained prescriptive requirements for the design and construction of steel moment-frame buildings. These requirements included specification of minimum permissible strength and stiffness for resisting earthquake loading, and specific requirements for connections between beams and columns. The Northridge earthquake demonstrated that some of these prescriptive requirements were not adequate. Following that discovery, the prescriptive requirements were removed from building codes used in regions of high earthquake risk and replaced with a requirement that designs include test data to show that reliable performance could be achieved for each new building. These new requirements were both costly and difficult to enforce and resulted in a decrease in the number of steel moment-frame buildings constructed.

Studies conducted under the FEMA/SAC program to reduce earthquake hazards in welded moment-resisting steel frames confirm that some of the design requirements contained in the building codes prior to the Northridge earthquake were inadequate. In the time since, some of these inadequate requirements have been improved based on interim findings and recommendations of the FEMA/SAC program. Now that the program is complete, *FEMA 350* presents a series of additional criteria for the design and construction of steel moment-frame buildings that should make performance of these structures in future earthquakes much more reliable. It is recommended that the building codes adopt these new recommendations and that, until this occurs, engineers and owners voluntarily adopt these criteria when developing new buildings.

What types of changes to design and construction practice does FEMA 350 recommend?

The *FEMA 350* recommendations affect nearly all phases of the design and construction process. The recommendations address the types of steel used, the way in which columns and beams are connected, the way the steel is fabricated, the type of welding that is performed, and the techniques that are used to assure that the construction work is performed properly.

In addition, *FEMA 350* provides engineers with a series of performance-based design criteria that can be used to design and construct buildings to resist earthquakes reliably while sustaining less damage than anticipated by building codes.

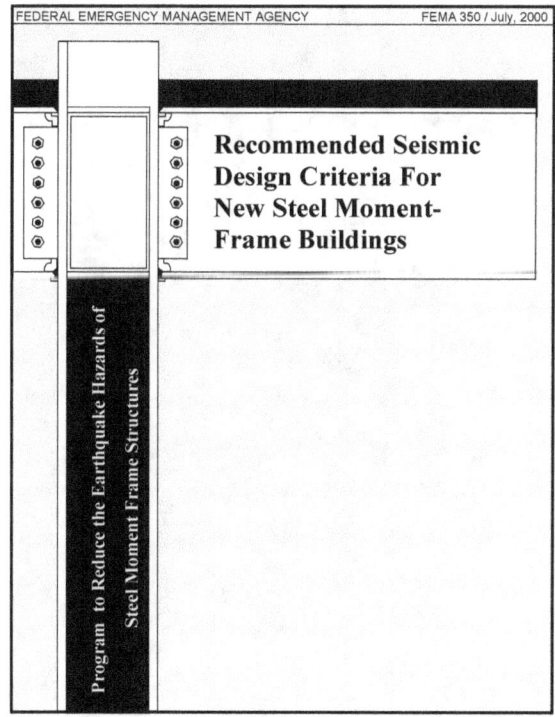

FEMA 350 provides recommendations for design and construction of new steel moment-frame buildings. These recommendations affect the materials of construction, design and construction procedures, and methods of quality assurance.

What are the recommended changes to the types of structural steel that should be used?

In the last few years, the steel industry in the United States has undergone rapid change with old rolling mills phased out and new mills, using more modern technologies, coming on line. Although the chemical composition and physical properties of steel have changed rapidly during this period, industry standard specifications and design practice largely neglected this. Working with the FEMA/SAC project, the American Institute of Steel Construction (AISC) developed new industry standard specifications for structural steel material. These new specifications provide better control of the critical properties that are important to earthquake performance. *FEMA 350* recommends the use of these more modern steels and also recommends design procedures that properly account for the high strength of modern steel materials.

Methods of steel production have undergone dramatic change in recent years and industry standard design and material production specifications did not adequately reflect the material currently produced. FEMA 350 updates the code requirements to assure specification of proper materials and proper treatment in design.

Are there any changes to welding requirements?

FEMA 350 and its companion document, *FEMA 353,* present extensive new recommendations for welding of moment-resisting connections in frames designed for seismic applications. The new recommendations address the types of materials that may be used for this work, the welding processes and procedures that should be followed, the environmental conditions under which welding should be performed, and the level of training and workmanship required of welders and inspectors engaged in this work. In addition, *FEMA 353* provides detailed recommendations for quality control, quality assurance and inspection procedures that should be put into place to assure that this critical work is properly performed. These new recommendations affect all segments of the design and construction process and require designers, producers, fabricators, welding electrode manufacturers, welders and inspectors, among others, to adopt new practices. These recommendations have been submitted to the American Welding Society for incorporation into the structural welding code.

If inadequately constructed, welded joints in moment-frames can be weak links that fail prematurely. FEMA 350 recommends careful control of the materials, workmanship and procedures used to make these joints and verify their adequacy.

What is different about the new design procedures?

Prior to the Northridge earthquake, most steel moment-frame designs used a standard connection that was prescribed by the building code. We know now that the configuration of these connections was problematic and resulted in unreliable connection performance. Following this discovery, the building codes were changed to require testing of each new connection design. This was very costly and difficult to implement. *FEMA 350* presents a series of new connection configurations that are recommended as prequalified for use in moment-frames conforming to certain limitations. The use of these prequalified connections will greatly simplify the design process and make the construction of new moment-frame buildings more economical and more reliable.

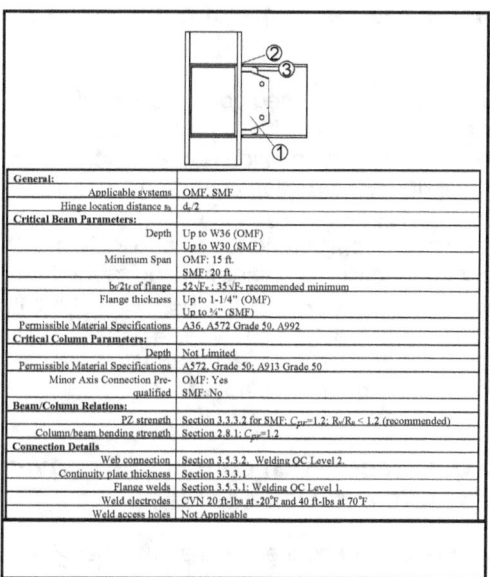

General:	
Applicable systems	OMF, SMF
Hinge location distance s_h	$d_c/2$
Critical Beam Parameters:	
Depth	Up to W36 (OMF)
	Up to W30 (SMF)
Minimum Span	OMF: 15 ft.
	SMF: 20 ft.
$b_f/2t_f$ of flange	$52\sqrt{F_y}$; $35\sqrt{F_y}$ recommended minimum
Flange thickness	Up to 1-1/4" (OMF)
	Up to ⅜" (SMF)
Permissible Material Specifications	A36, A572 Grade 50, A992
Critical Column Parameters:	
Depth	Not Limited
Permissible Material Specifications	A572, Grade 50; A913 Grade 50
Minor Axis Connection Pre-qualified	OMF: Yes
	SMF: No
Beam/Column Relations:	
PZ strength	Section 3.3.3.2 for SMF; $C_{pr}=1.2$; $R_y/R_t < 1.2$ (recommended)
Column/beam bending strength	Section 2.8.1; $C_{pr}=1.2$
Connection Details	
Web connection	Section 3.5.3.2. Welding QC Level 2.
Continuity plate thickness	Section 3.3.3.1
Flange welds	Section 3.5.3.1; Welding QC Level 1.
Weld electrodes	CVN 20 ft-lbs at -20°F and 40 ft-lbs at 70°F
Weld access holes	Not Applicable

FEMA 350 provides prescriptive criteria for prequalified beam-to-column connections capable of reliable performance.

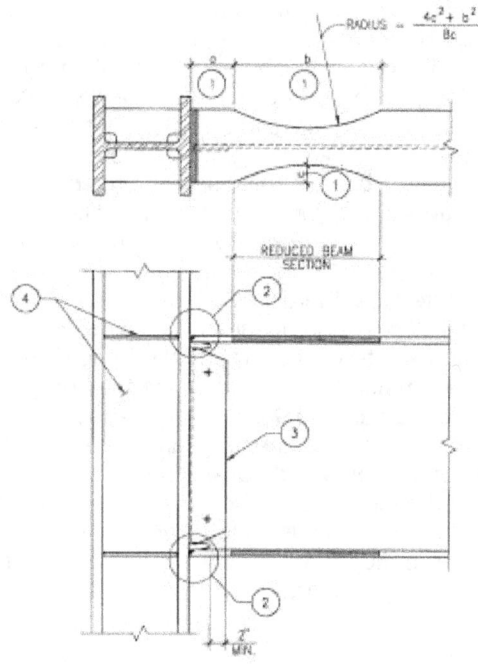

The Reduced Beam Section, or "dog bone" connection is one of 12 different types of prequalified connections that engineers can specify without project-specific testing.

How many different types of connections are prequalified?

FEMA 350 contains design criteria for twelve different types of prequalified, welded and bolted beam-to-column connections. Each prequalification includes specification of the limiting conditions under which the connection design is valid, the materials that may be used, and the specific design and fabrication requirements.

What is the basis for the new prequalified connections?

The new prequalified connections contained in *FEMA 350* are based on extensive laboratory and analytical investigations including more than 120 full-scale tests of beam-to-column connection assemblies and numerous analytical studies of the behavior of different connection types. Connections were prequalified only after their behavior was understood, analytical models were developed that could predict this behavior and laboratory testing demonstrated that the connections would behave reliably.

What is the best type of connection to use?

Each of the prequalified connections offers certain advantages with regard to design considerations, fabrication and erection complexity, construction cost, and structural performance capability. No one connection type will be most appropriate for all applications. It is likely that individual engineers and fabricators will develop preferences for the use of specific types of connections, and that certain connections will see widespread use in some parts of the country but not others.

Do the prequalified connections cover all possible design cases?

The prequalifed connections should be applicable to many common design conditions. However, they are not universally applicable to all structures and, in particular, are limited in applicability with regard to the size, types and orientation of framing members with which they can be used. If a design requires the use of types or sizes of framing that are not included in the ranges for a prequalified connection, *FEMA 350* recommends that supplemental testing of the connection be performed to demonstrate that it will be capable of performing adequately.

Is it possible to use types of connections other than those that are prequalified?

FEMA 350 contains information on several types of proprietary connections that are not prequalified and nothing in *FEMA 350* prevents engineers from developing or using other types of connection designs. However, *FEMA 350* does state that, when other types of connections are used, a testing program should be conducted to demonstrate that these connections can perform adequately. *FEMA 350* also presents information on the types of testing that should be conducted and how to determine if connection performance is acceptable.

Will designs employing these new recommendations cost more?

The cost of a steel frame building is generally dependent on the amount of labor required to fabricate and erect the steel and the total number of tons of steel in the building frame. The new design recommendations both formalize and simplify design procedures that generally have been in use by engineers since the 1994 Northridge earthquake. They do not result in an increase in steel tonnage or significantly greater labor for fabrication and erection. However, more extensive construction quality assurance measures are recommended and these will result in some additional construction cost. It is anticipated that this additional cost will amount to less than 1% of the total construction cost for typical buildings.

Will buildings designed to the new recommendations be earthquake proof?

It is theoretically possible to design and construct buildings that are strong enough to resist severe earthquakes without damage, but it would not be economical to do so and we could not afford to construct many such buildings. The objective of most building codes is to design buildings such that they might be damaged by severe earthquakes but not collapse and endanger occupants in any earthquake they are likely to experience. The *FEMA 350* recommendations adopt this same design philosophy. It is anticipated that there would be a very low risk of life threatening damage in buildings designed and constructed in accordance with the *FEMA 350* recommendations. However, they may experience damage that will require repair, including permanent bending and yielding of the framing elements and possible permanent lateral drift of the structure. Although it is possible that some connections designed using the new procedure may fracture, it is anticipated that this will not be widespread.

Will the new recommendations be included in the building codes?

The seismic provisions of current building codes are largely based on the *NEHRP Recommended Provisions for Seismic Regulations of Buildings and Other Structures*, supplemented by standard specifications developed by industry associations, including the American Institute of Steel Construction (AISC) and the American Welding Society (AWS). Many of the design recommendations contained in *FEMA 350* have already been incorporated into the standard design specifications developed by AISC and are directly referenced by the 2000 *International Building Code*. The remaining recommendations are being proposed for incorporation into later editions of the AISC and AWS specifications. This material is also being included in the *NEHRP Recommended Provisions for Seismic Regulations of New Buildings and Other Structures*. Some of the earlier material has already been included in the 1997 edition (*FEMA 302/303*) and the remainder of the material will be incorporated into the new 2000 edition (*FEMA 368/369*), due to be released in spring 2001. It is anticipated that many jurisdictions around the United States will adopt building codes based on these criteria as the basis for building regulation in their communities.

Is it possible to design to the new recommendations before the new building codes are adopted?

Many of the new design recommendations are compatible with existing building code regulations that are already in force around the United States. It should be possible for engineers to utilize the new recommendations, on a voluntary basis, as a supplement to the existing building code requirements. However, the local building official is the ultimate authority as to the acceptability of this practice. Engineers should verify that the building official will accept the new documents prior to using them to design buildings.

Is it possible to design for better performance?

As an option, *FEMA 350* includes a methodology which engineers can use to design for superior performance relative to that anticipated by the building code. This approach is similar to the procedures contained in *FEMA 351* for the evaluation and upgrade of existing buildings. In these procedures, a decision must be made as to what level of performance is desired for a specific level of earthquake motion. As an example, one of the available performance levels, termed Immediate Occupancy, results in such slight damage that the building should be available for occupancy immediately following the earthquake. The performance-based procedures of *FEMA 350* can be used to design a building such that there is a high probability the building will provide Immediate Occupancy performance for any level of earthquake intensity that is desired. As a minimum, however, buildings should be designed to satisfy the prescriptive criteria of the applicable building code, which are intended to protect life safety.

CONSTRUCTION QUALITY CONTROL AND ASSURANCE

What is construction quality control?

Construction quality control includes that set of actions taken by the contractor to ensure that construction conforms to the specified material and workmanship standards, the requirements of the design drawings and the applicable building code. Construction quality control includes hiring workers and subcontractors that have the necessary training and experience to perform the construction properly; making sure that these workers understand the project requirements and their responsibility to execute them; and performing routine inspections and tests to confirm that the work is properly performed. Some contractors may retain independent inspection and testing agencies to assist them with their quality control functions.

What is construction quality assurance?

Construction quality assurance is that set of actions, including inspections, observations and tests, that are performed on the owner's behalf to ensure that the contractor is conforming to the design and building code requirements. In essence, construction quality assurance represents a second line of defense and supplements the contractor's own quality control program. Building codes specify minimum levels of quality assurance for different types of construction. If the contractor on a project does not perform adequate quality control it may be appropriate to provide more quality assurance than required by the applicable building code. Quality assurance tasks are typically performed by design professionals and special inspection and testing agencies specifically retained by the owner for this purpose. It is recommended that the engineer assist the owner in determining the level of quality assurance appropriate to a specific project, and also that the engineer be retained by the owner to actively monitor and participate in the quality assurance process.

Why is construction quality control and quality assurance important?

Investigations performed after every earthquake indicate that much of the damage that occurs is a result of structures not being constructed in accordance with the applicable building code or the designer's intent. This problem has affected nearly every type of building construction, including wood frame, masonry, concrete and steel buildings. Construction errors and construction work that is improperly performed create weak links where damage in structures can initiate. Earthquakes can place extreme loading on structures and, if structures contain improper construction, damage is likely to occur where that poor construction occurs.

Was inadequate construction quality a significant factor in the damage sustained by steel buildings in the Northridge earthquake?

One of the contributors to the damage sustained by steel moment-frame buildings in the Northridge earthquake was construction that did not conform to the applicable standards. In particular, investigations conducted after the earthquake revealed that critical welds of beams to columns were not made in accordance with the building code requirements. A number of defects were commonly found in the construction including: welds that had large slag inclusions and lack of fusion (bonding) with the steel columns, welds that were placed too quickly and with too much heat input into the joint; and welding aids including backing and weld tabs that were improperly installed. These construction defects resulted in welded joints that had lower strength and toughness than should have been provided, resulting in a propensity for damage.

Who is responsible for construction quality control and assurance?

Each of the participants in building construction, including the design engineer, the contractor, the building official, and special inspectors, plays a critical role in assuring that construction meets the appropriate standards. The engineer must specify the applicable standards and the quality assurance measures that are to be used. The contractor must perform the work in the required manner and perform inspections to verify that this occurs. Building codes require that the owner retain a special inspection agency to perform detailed inspections and assure that the contractor is executing the work properly. The responsible building official typically monitors the entire process and makes sure that each of the parties fulfills their individual responsibilities.

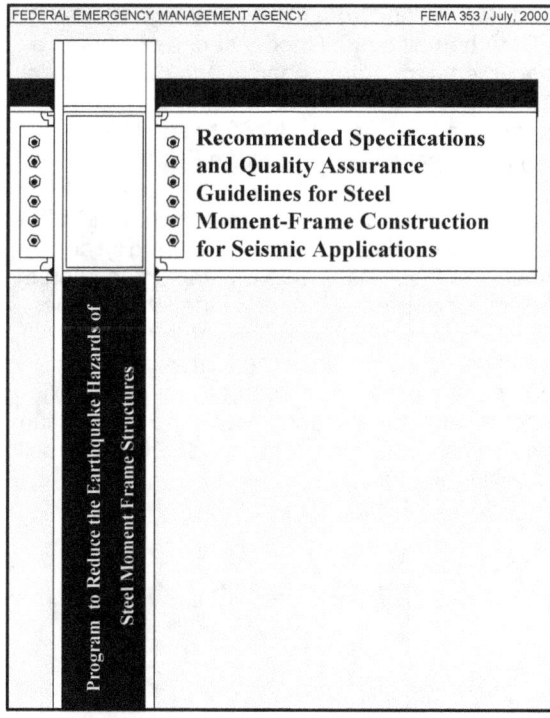

FEDERAL EMERGENCY MANAGEMENT AGENCY   FEMA 353 / July, 2000

Recommended Specifications and Quality Assurance Guidelines for Steel Moment-Frame Construction for Seismic Applications

Program to Reduce the Earthquake Hazards of Steel Moment Frame Structures

FEMA 353 provides recommended specifications for fabrication, erection, and quality assurance of steel moment-frame structures designed for seismic applications.

Where can one find recommendations on appropriate quality control and quality assurance procedures?

FEMA 353 provides detailed recommendations for procedures that should be followed to assure that steel moment-frame construction complies with the applicable standards. It includes information that is useful to engineers, building officials, contractors and inspectors. This information is presented in the form of specifications that can be included in the project specifications developed by engineers for specific projects. It also includes commentary that explains the basis for the recommendations and methods that can be used to implement them.

Are the new quality recommendations significantly different than those required in the past?

Many of the recommendations contained in *FEMA 353* are a restatement and clarification of requirements already contained in building codes and in the standard AISC and AWS specifications. There are also some important new recommendations. These include new requirements intended to assure that weld filler metals and welding procedures are capable of providing welded joints of adequate strength and toughness. In addition, comprehensive recommendations are provided as to the extent of testing and inspection that should be performed on different welded joints. In part, these new requirements are based on findings that the inspection methods traditionally used in the past to assure weld quality are incapable of reliably detecting nonconforming construction. It is anticipated that many of these new requirements will be incorporated into the AWS standards in the future.

PREPARING FOR THE NEXT EARTHQUAKE

What should communities do before the next disaster occurs?

Before the next disaster strikes, communities should conduct a thorough examination of their vulnerability to natural hazards and the risks they may present to their citizens. In addition to a potential earthquake threat, communities may be vulnerable to other significant hazards, such as flooding, high winds, hurricanes, tornadoes, tsunami, etc. While this publication addresses the potential earthquake risk of steel moment-frame buildings, communities may have more significant risks from other more hazardous types of buildings, such as unreinforced masonry, non-ductile concrete frame or tilt-up concrete buildings. Communities should carefully consider all of these potential risks and how they may affect the different types of construction present.

Regardless of the risk posed by existing construction, before the next disaster occurs communities should adopt reliable building codes and building regulation practices that will ensure that new buildings are adequately designed and constructed to resist the future earthquakes and other disasters that will inevitably occur. Building codes that incorporate the latest edition of the *NEHRP Recommended Provisions for Seismic Regulation for Buildings and Other Structures* are strongly recommended.

Communities may wish to encourage building owners to upgrade their existing hazardous buildings to minimize potential damage, economic and life loss. *FEMA 351* can be used as a technical basis for both voluntary and mandatory upgrade programs. In addition, communities should put emergency response systems into place. Building departments should train their personnel to conduct building inspections. In large cities, building departments will quickly become overwhelmed by this responsibility. Before the next earthquake, the building department should make arrangements for assistance from outside the affected area. Some states have agencies that will facilitate this. Communities should also consider adopting ordinances to govern the post-earthquake building inspection and repair process. Experience has shown that some building owners will not act responsibly to inspect and repair buildings, unless required by law to do so. FEMA 352 can be used as a basis for developing post-earthquake inspection and repair ordinances.

Is help available?

FEMA has developed a number of tools that communities can use to identify their exposure to natural disasters, including both earthquake and flood hazard maps. FEMA has also developed standardized, GIS-based computer software that can help a community to assess the risk that these hazards present. This software package, called HazardsUS, or HAZUS, presently addresses earthquake risk, however modules are currently under development that will also address the risk from floods and high winds. FEMA has also published a series of guidance documents for both technical and non-technical audiences to assist in addressing specific hazard-related issues. All of these aids are available, without charge, from FEMA.

Once the hazard and risk are known, FEMA has a community-based initiative called Project Impact to help encourage the implementation of pre-disaster prevention, or mitigation, activities. This initiative, which may include a one-time seed grant, encourages the formation of community-based partnerships between public and private stakeholders. For more information on this and other programs, visit FEMA's website at www.fema.gov.

Project Impact assists communities to form public and private partnerships to reduce the potential for natural disaster losses.

THE FEMA/SAC PROJECT AND DISSEMINATING ITS RESULTS

Why did FEMA elect to undertake such an effort?

FEMA, as part of its role in the National Earthquake Hazards Reduction Program (NEHRP), is charged with reducing the ever-increasing cost of damage in earthquakes. Preventing losses before they happen, or mitigation, is the only truly effective way of reducing this cost. In this light, the role of this nation's building codes and standards in mitigating earthquake losses is critical, and FEMA is committed to working with this nation's seismic codes and standards to keep them among the best in the world. Because the damage that resulted from the Northridge earthquake called into question the design assumptions and building code requirements associated with steel moment-frame construction and because of the unknown life safety hazard of the damaged buildings, it was crucial that adequate repair and retrofitting procedures be quickly identified. This was particularly critical for FEMA, because many of the damaged steel buildings were publicly owned and therefore the cost of damage repair was eligible for funding under the public assistance provisions of the Robert T. Stafford Disaster Relief and Emergency Assistance Act. To fully respond to this need, development of reliable and cost-effective methods for use in the various building codes and standards that address the design of new construction and the repair and/or upgrading of existing steel moment-frame buildings was necessary.

The solution of this problem required a coordinated, problem-focused program of research, investigation and professional development with the goal of developing and validating reliable and cost-effective seismic-resistant design procedures for steel moment-frame structures. This work involved consideration of many complex technical, professional and economic issues including metallurgy, welding, fracture mechanics, connection behavior, system performance, and practices related to design, fabrication, erection and inspection.

How were related policy issues addressed by the FEMA/SAC project?

As part of the project, an expert panel with representation from the financial, legal, commercial real estate, construction, and building regulation communities was formed to review social, economic, legal and political issues related to the technical recommendations. This panel was charged with evaluating the potential impact of the recommended design and construction criteria on various stakeholder groups, identifying potential barriers to effective implementation of the recommendations and advising the project team on potential ways of making the guidelines more useful and effective. The panel held a workshop in October 1997 that brought together representatives of these constituencies, and their recommendations were considered during the development of technical recommendations and in the preparation of this publication.

Why did it take so long to develop the necessary information?

The damage experienced by steel moment-frame structures in the Northridge earthquake called to question the entire portions of building codes that addressed this type of construction, and which had been developed over a period of more than 20 years. This project basically had to start from scratch and either revalidate all of the existing criteria, or when this criteria was found to be inadequate, develop new design criteria and construction standards that could be relied upon. This involved a complete re-evaluation of the properties of structural steels and welding materials, the assumptions used in designing and evaluating different types of moment-connections, and the methods used in inspecting and evaluating these connections and their behavior. In the process, all of this material had to be developed and presented in a rigorous and scientifically defensible manner so that it would be recognized as reliable and used by the building design, construction and regulatory communities. This project accomplished in six years what originally evolved over 20 years.

How will this information be put unto practice?

The new FEMA guidance documents are now being widely disseminated to the structural engineering and building regulation communities. Three of these publications provide recommended criteria for design of more reliable new construction (*FEMA 350*), upgrading existing structures to minimize the potential for future damage (*FEMA 351*), and evaluating and repairing buildings after an earthquake (*FEMA 352*). The fourth provides technical specifications and quality assurance guidelines (*FEMA 353*). Much of the information contained in these publications, especially for new construction, is being incorporated into both the *NEHRP Recommended Provisions for Seismic Regulation of Buildings and Other Structures* and the latest standard design specification published by AISC. Together, these publications serve as the consensus design standard for steel structures nationwide. This standard is routinely adopted by reference into the model building codes where it is in turn used as part of state and/or local building codes. AISC has also published a design guide, developed jointly with NIST, for upgrade of existing structures, and which compliments the recommendations contained in *FEMA 351*.

How can one obtain additional information?

The four FEMA publications described above can be ordered free of charge by calling 1-800-480-2520. In addition, a series of state-of-the-art reports have been developed which summarize the current state of knowledge that forms the technical basis for the recommended criteria publications. These reports are available from FEMA in CD-ROM format (*FEMA 355*). Individual reports on the technical investigations performed in support of the FEMA/SAC project are available as well. These technical reports and *FEMA 355* may be purchased in hard copy format from the SAC Joint Venture. The SAC Joint Venture will also continue to maintain a publicly accessible site on the World Wide Web at www.sacsteel.org. Future information and training opportunities will be available from the American Institute of Steel Construction (AISC) and other organizations. Consult AISC's World Wide Web site at www.aisc.org for additional information.

INDEX

The term "mitigation" describes actions which can help reduce or eliminate your long-term risk from natural disasters. With mitigation, you can avoid losses and reduce your risk of becoming a disaster victim.

There are many low-cost mitigation measures you can take to protect yourself, your home, or your business from losses. For example:

FLOODING

- Move valuables and appliances out of the basement of your home or business if it is prone to flooding. This will increase the chance that your belongings will remain dry when a flood occurs.

- Have the main breaker or fuse-box and the utility meters elevated above the anticipated flood level in your home or business, so that flood water won't damage your utilities.

- Buy flood insurance to cover the value of your home and its contents. Not only will it give you greater peace of mind, but it will also greatly speed your recovery if a flood occurs. To learn more about flood insurance, contact your insurance company or agent, or call 1-800-427-4661.

EARTHQUAKES

- Bolt or strap cupboards and bookcases to the wall, and keep heavy objects on the lower shelves. This will reduce both damages and the possibility of injury to those in your home or business.

- Strap your water heater to a nearby wall using bands of perforated steel (commonly known as "plumber's tape"). If a gas water heater falls during an earthquake, it could break the gas line and start a fire.

- Install bolts to support your home to its foundation. Anchor bolts cost as little as $2 a piece, but can prevent thousands of dollars of damage. Have them installed every six feet around the perimeter of your home.

HAZARD MITIGATION WORKS, AND IT CAN SAVE YOU MONEY. IT HELPS PROTECT YOUR FAMILY, YOUR BUSINESS AND YOUR PROPERTY FROM THE EFFECTS OF NATURAL DISASTERS.

HURRICANES AND TORNADOES

- Have hurricane straps installed in your home or business to better secure the roof to the walls and foundation. This will reduce the risk of losing your roof to high winds.

- Install and maintain storm shutters to protect all exposed windows and glass surfaces, and use them when severe weather threatens. Besides protecting against wind, shutters also prevent damage from flying debris.

- Have your home inspected by a building professional to ensure that roof and other building components are capable of withstanding wind effects.

WILDFIRES

- Move shrubs and other landscaping away from the sides of your house or deck. All too often, homes burn when plantings around them catch fire.

- Install tile or flame-retardant shingles on your roof, instead of wood shakes or standard shingles. This will reduce the chance that airborne burning debris will end up destroying your home.

- Clear dead brush and grass from your property so that it will not provide fuel for a spreading fire.

Is your family, home, or business protected from natural disasters?

They can be.

REDUCE YOUR RISK FROM NATURAL DISASTERS

Federal Emergency Management Agency

Reach us on the Internet at http://www.fema.gov

MAKE SURE TO MITIGATE PROPERLY — THE FIRST TIME!

Most communities have building codes and ordinances which guide construction practices. Many of these are designed to reduce your risk from all types of hazards, including floods, earthquakes, high winds, and wildfires.

If you have any questions about local codes or ordinances, and how they may impact mitigation efforts in your home or business, contact a professional or your building official. Either should be able to provide you with the assistance you need to mitigate right the first time.

Mitigation Begins With You — Learn to Build Stronger, Safer, Smarter!

To learn more about hazard mitigation measures that you can take to reduce your risk from disasters, visit FEMA's Internet site (www.fema.gov), or call 1-800-480-2520 to have a list of available mitigation publications mailed to your home or office.

You can also contact the FEMA Regional Office nearest you:

FEMA Region I (serving CT, NH, ME, MA, RI, VT)
J.W. McCormack Post Office
Courthouse Bldg., Rm. 442
Boston, MA 02109   tel: (617) 223-9540

FEMA Region II (serving NJ, NY, PR, VI)
26 Federal Plaza, Rm. 1337
New York, NY 10278   tel: (212) 225-7209

FEMA Region III (serving DC, DE, MD, PA, VA, WV)
Liberty Square Bldg., 2nd Floor
105 S. Seventh St.
Philadelphia, PA 19106   tel: (215) 931-5608

FEMA Region IV (serving AL, FL, GA, KY, MS, NC, SC, TN)
Koger Center - Rutgers Bldg.
3003 Chamblee-Tucker Road
Atlanta, GA 30341   tel: (770) 220-5200

FEMA Region V (serving IL, IN, OH, MN, WI)
175 W. Jackson Blvd. 4th Floor
Chicago, IL 60604   tel: (312) 408-5518

FEMA Region VI (serving AR, LA, NM, OK, TX)
Federal Regional Center
800 N. Loop
Denton, TX 76201   tel: (817) 898-5127

FEMA Region VII (serving IA, KS, MO, NE)
2323 Grand Blvd., Ste. 900
Kansas City, MO 64108   tel: (816) 283-7066

FEMA Region VIII (serving CO, MT, ND, SD, UT, WY)
Denver Federal Center Bldg. 710
Box 25267
Denver, CO 80225   tel: (303) 235-4830

FEMA Region IX (serving AZ, CA, HI, NV)
Building 105, the Presidio
San Francisco, CA 94129   tel: (415) 923-7177

FEMA Region X (serving AK, ID, OR, WA)
Federal Regional Center
130 228th St., SW
Bothell, WA 98021   tel: (206) 481-8800

FEDERAL EMERGENCY MANAGEMENT AGENCY
SEISMIC SAFETY OF BUILDINGS

> *Sources of information for design professionals and other decision makers in earthquake hazard mitigation*

EXISTING BUILDINGS

Rapid Visual Screening of Buildings for Potential Seismic Hazards: A Handbook (FEMA-I 54, 1988, 185 pages) and ***Rapid Visual Screening of Buildings for Potential Seismic Hazards: Supporting Documentation*** **(FEMA-I 55,1988,137 pages).** Prepared by the Applied Technology Council, Redwood City, CA (ATC-21 and ATC-21 -1).

The Handbook presents a method for quickly identifying buildings posing risk of death, injury, or severe curtailment in use following an earthquake. The methodology, "Rapid Screening Procedure (RSP)," can be used by trained personnel to identify potentially hazardous buildings on the basis of a 15 to 30 minute exterior inspection, using a data collection form included in the Handbook. Twelve basic structural categories are inspected, leading to a numerical "structural score" based on visual inspection. Building inspectors are the most likely group to implement an RSP, although this report is also intended for building officials, engineers, architects, building owners, emergency managers and interested citizens. The Supporting Documentation reviews the literature and existing procedures for rapid visual screening.

NEHRP Handbook for the Seismic Evaluation of Existing Buildings (FEMA-178, 1992, 227 pages). Prepared by the Building **Seismic Safety Council, Washington, D.C.**

The Handbook presents a nationally applicable method for engineers to identify buildings or building components that present unacceptable risks in case of an earthquake. Four structural subsystems in which deficits may exist are identified: vertical elements resisting horizontal loads; horizontal elements resisting lateral loads; foundations; and connections between structural elements or subsystems. Fifteen structural categories are defined for the evaluation of buildings by engineers. The Handbook is formulated to be compatible with NEHRP Handbook of Techniques for the Seismic Rehabilitation of Existing Buildings (FEMA-172/1992).

NEHRP Handbook of Techniques for the Seismic Rehabilitation of Existing Buildings (FEMA-172, 1992,197 pages). Prepared by the Building Seismic Safety Council, Washington, DC.

This handbook presents techniques for solving a variety of seismic rehabilitation problems. intended for engineers concerned with seismic rehabilitation of existing buildings, the handbook identifies and describes seismic rehabilitation techniques for a broad spectrum of building types and building components (both structural and nonstructural). Most techniques are illustrated with sketches, and the relative merits of the techniques are discussed. Designed to be compatible with the NEHRP Handbook for the Seismic Evaluation of Existing Buildings (FEMA-178/1992), this publication is based on a prelimary version prepared by URS/John A. Blume and Associates, Technique for Seismically Rehabilitating Existing Buildings (FEMA-172/1989).

Typical Costs for Seismic Rehabilitation of Existing Buildings: Volume 1: Summary, Second Edition (FEMA-156, 1994, approx. 70 pages); ***Volume 2: Supporting Documentation, Second Edition*** (FEMA-1 57, 1995,approx. 102 pages). Prepared by the Hart Consultant Group, Inc. Santa Monica, CA. [FEMA-156, 1994 **AND FEMA-157, 1995 SUPERSEDE FEMA-156, 1988 AND FEMA-157. 1988].**

*Typical Costa for Seismic Rehabilitation of Existing Buildings: Volume I: Summary second Edition*provides a methodology that enables users to estimate the costs of seismic rehabilitation projects at various locations in the United States. This greatly improved edition is based on a sample of almost 2100 projects. The data were collected by use of a standard protocol, given a stringent quality control verification and a reliability rating, and then entered into a database that is available to practitioners. A sophisticated statistical methodology applied to this database yields costs estimates of increasing quality and reliability as more and more detailed information on the building inventory is used in the estimation process. Guidance is also provided to calculate a range of uncertainty associated with this process. The Supporting Documentation contains an in-depth discussion of the approaches and methodology that were used in developing the second edition.

Benefit-Cost Model for the Seismic Rehabilitation of Hazardous Buildings. Volume *1: A User's* Manual (FEMA-227, 1992, approx. 68 pages); *Volume 2: Supporting Documentation (FEMA-228, 1992, approx. 62 pages);* and **Computer Software for Benefit-Cost Model for the Seismic Rehabilifation of Hazardous Buildings.** Prepared by VSP Associates, Inc., Sacramento, CA.

The two benefit-cost models presented in this report are designed to help evaluate the economic benefits and costs of seismic rehabilitation of existing hazardous buildings. The single class model analyzes groups of buildings with a single structural type, a single use, and a single set of economic assumptions. The multi-class model analyzes groups of buildings that may have several structural types and uses. The User's manual presents background information on the development of the benefit-cost model and an introduction to the use of benefit/cost analysis in decision making. It reviews the economic assumptions of benefit-cost models, with and without including the value of life. The User's Manual guides the user through the model by presenting synopses of data entries required, example model results, and supporting information. Seven applications of the models are presented: five of the single-class model; two of the multi-class model.

Supporting Documentation complements the User's Manual by providing four appendices that help the user understand how the benefit-cost models were constructed. The appendices include: 1) a review of relevant literature; 2) a section on estimating costs for seismic rehabilitation; 3) a compilation of tables for the Seattle building inventory; and 4) some insights into the building rehabilitation of the nine cities visited during this project.

Computer Software to run the benefit/cost models is also available. The programs are on 3½" diskettes and can be used on IBM compatible personal computers.

Seismic Rehabilitation of Federal Buildings: A Benefit/ Cost Model. Volume 1: A User's Manual (FEMA 255,1994, approx. 158 pages); *Volume 2: Supporting Documentation (FEMA-256, 1994,* approx. 71 pages) and **Computer Software for the Seismic Rehabilitation of Federal Buildings.** Prepared by VSP Associates, **Inc., Sacramento, CA.**

This User's **Manuel** and accompanying software present a second generation cost-benefit model for the seismic rehabilitation of federal and other government buildings. Intended for facility managers, design professionals, and others involved in decision making, the cost/benefit methodology provides estimates of the benefits (avoided damages, avoided losses, and avoided casualties) of seismic rehabilitation, as well as estimates of the costs necessary to implement the rehabilitation. The methodology also generates detailed scenario estimates of damages, losses, and casualties. The **Manual** describes the computer hardware and software required to run the program. It also explains how to install the program, how to use Quattro Pro for Windows, and how to enter necessary data. A tutorial provides a fully worked example. Benefit/Cost analyses of eight federal buildings are included. The Supporting Documentation contains background information for the **User's Manual** including information on valuing public sector services, discount rates and multipliers, the dollar value of human life, and technical issues that affect benefit/cost analysis, such as seismic risk assessment and sensitivity analysis.

Computer Software to run the benefit/cost model is available on 3 1/2" diskettes and can be used on IBM compatible personal computers with at least 386 CPU. The computer must also have Windows and Quattro Pro.

Establishing Programs and Priorities for the Seismic Rehabilitation of Buildings: handbook(FEMA-174,1989,122 pages) and **Establishing Programs and Priorities for the Seismic Rehabilitation of Buildings: Supporting Report** (FEMA-173, 1989, 190 pages). Prepared by Building *Systems* Development, Inc. with integrated Design Services and Claire B. Rubin.

These two **volumes** provide the information needed to develop a seismic rehabilitation? program, with particular reference establishing priorities. The Handbook is intended to assist local jurisdictions in making informed decisions on rehabilitating seismically hazardous existing buildings by providing nationally applicable guidelines. It discusses the pertinent issues that merit consideration, both technical and societal, and suggests a procedure whereby these issues can be resolved. The Supporting Report includes additional information and commentary directly related **to sections in** the Handbook supporting documentation, annotated bibliographies, and reproductions of selected laws and ordinances that are presented in summary form **in the Handbook.**

Financial Incentives for Seismic Rehabilitation of Hazardous Buildings - An Agenda for Action. Volume 1: Findings, Conclusions, and Recommendations (FEMA-198, 1990,104 pages); *Volume 2: State and Local Case Studies and Recommendations* (FEMA-199, 1990, 130 pages); and *Volume 3: Applications Workshops Report* (FEMA-216, 1990, about 200 pages). **Prepared by Building Technology, Inc., Silver Spring, MD.**

The **intent** of these documents is to identify and describe the existing and potential regulatory and financial mechanisms and incentives for lessening the risks posed by existing buildings in an earthquake. **Volume 1** includes a discussion of the methodology used for these documents, background information on financial incentives, as well as findings, conclusions and recommendations for use by decision makers at local, state and national levels. **Volume 2 includes detailed descriptions of the twenty case studies that were examined as part of this project. Volume** 3 reports on workshops for the development of local agendas for action in seismic rehabilitation. It includes directions for convening additional workshops and teaching materials which can be used in such workshops. This information is directed primarily to groups that are interested in planning for local seismic mitigation in existing buildings who wish to convene a workshop to initiate the process.

***Development of Guidelines for Seismic Rehabilitation of
Buildings - Phase 1: issues identification and Resolution
(FEMA-237,* November 1992, 150 pages). Prepared by the
Applied Technology Council, Redwood City CA (ATC-28).**

This report is intended to assist in the preparation of Guide-
**lines for the Seismic Rehabilitation of Existing Buildings.
The** report identifies and analyzes issues that may impact
the preparation of the **Guidelines** and offers alternative as
well as recommended solutions to facilitate their development and implementation. Also discussed are issues concerned with the scope, implementation, and format of the
Guidelines, as well as coordination efforts, and legal, political, social, and economic aspects. Issues concerning his-
toric buildings, research and new technology, seismicity and
mapping, as well as engineering philosophy and goals are
discussed. The report concludes with a presentation of issues concerned with the development of specific provisions
for major structural and nonstructural elements.

Publications concerning ***existing buildings*** can be obtained at no charge from the FEMA Distribution Center, P.O. Box 2012, Jessup,
MD 20794. Telephone: 1-800-480-2520; Fax: (301) 497-6378.

This list was prepared by the **Information Service,** National Center for Earthquake Engineering Research **(NCEER), 304 Capen Hall,**
University at Buffalo, Buffalo, NY 14260-2200. Telephone: (716) 645-3377; Fax: (716) 645-3379;
E-Mail: nernceer@ ubvms.cc.buffalo.edu; WWW: http://nceer.eng.buffalo.edu.   Revised 10/20/95